The Long Way Home

Sir Jvmes

BookLeaf
Publishing

India | USA | UK

Presentation by *BookLeaf Publishing*

Web: www.bookleafpub.com

E-mail: info@bookleafpub.com

ISBN: 9789357612906

First edition 2023

ACKNOWLEDGEMENT

I have to start by thanking my dear friend Firdose Khan for inspiring and encouraging me to finish the book when I was struggling - just so she could read it :) And for lending her National Geographic Rarely Seen: Photographs of the Extraordinary, which helped me fall in love with nature all over again and gave me that final push.

I would also like to thank my dear friends Farida Elgharably, Peace Olusanya, and Obed Darkwa for their support throughout the creation of these poems. Writing an anthology is one thing; writing all of the individual poems that comprise the anthology is quite another. A couple of the poems took a huge toll on me, but these friends were there to pick me up.

Finally, I would like to thank my dear friend Tahiya Abidha for always being there for me, through it all, and for her support with the front cover design.

Kudos - author's image captured by the G.O.A.T. @dreslenses

PREFACE

I wouldn't say I was heartbroken, but it's always sad when good things end. It was quiet when the end came for me. The kind of quiet you get when you've had a fantastic day out and are tired but excited to get home. We are constantly exposed to nature when we are outside, so I wanted to use it as a symbol for my experiences, a reference point to which everyone can relate.

My biggest challenge was providing context in such a way that it told an overall story while not detracting from the middle section, which focuses on the various elements of nature, and having it all cut from the same ribbon.

The purpose of this book is to encourage us to embrace everything there is and everything we experience, but also to demonstrate that the same thing can have multiple interpretations, that there is good in bad and bad in good, and that my friend… is life.

show love is red, i'm tired of blue

love comes in pairs it's
me and you. if love is on
top, show me the view

I Wander

I wandered lonely as a cloud in the sky trying to
figure everything out.
I danced with the stars and made love to the
moon
All whilst trying not to get burnt by the sun.
It's easy to lose yourself when you're looking for
somebody else.
Love is a gamble, a 4 letter word that can make
or break you
Place your bet, roll your die,
Because in the end, we are all just a bunch of
dreamers in an endless universe.

Until Next Time

You never claimed to be anybody special,
But there was nobody interesting left
When I found myself placed with you.
For the first time I concluded that I'd never been
happier.
I don't know what it was,
Something in our personalities perhaps
Where what was good was never in the slightest
doubt.
I hadn't imagined this, you're always on my
mind
See if you can come up with one good reason to
stick around,
If only there was some sign,
When the present seems unstable and the future
unlikely.
But it's too late, always has been, always will be
too late.
After each long kiss, you placed a smaller,
gentler one upon my lips like a signature.
Wait, before you leave, here - take these off
I want to see you.
And - and I want to be straight
I can't run from it, I care about you,
Please! Don't leave.
I really think there's hope, don't you?

I wish I could've let you know
But all of a sudden nobody can think of anything
to say.
Everybody knows what eventually became of
the silhouette.
All we ever see of stars are their old photographs
But I understood, at the end I understood,
Everything evens out eventually.

4,344

4,344.
That's how many miles there were between.
My legs had taken steps too many to count and I split into two.
Putting my best foot forward I continued with the better version of myself
And made my way to what I thought was my better half, you.
What I failed to realise was two halves don't make a whole if those halves do not align,
And someone should've told me searching for your other half is impossible because we were made whole.
So it's either you love the whole of me or none of me at all.
Why would you want one circle when you can have two?
If one were to ever stop rolling
The other is right behind pushing it forward,
But I was naive and I learnt this a little too late

4,344.
That's how many miles there were between.
A road formed a black ribbon cutting through my surroundings

And as beautiful as they were, I had not yet
learnt to stop and smell the flowers.
My heart longed for you and would not quit till
there I was, by your side.
But you made it hard,
I eventually concluded that it's not my body
that's tired but my soul.

Then there you were,
4,344 miles later and you gave me hope,
Or rather sold me a dream
After all, hope, isn't that what dreams are made
of?
So I made my way back home.

It's a Bit Windy

You were wind.
The sounds of smooth jazz whispering sweet
nothings into my ear.
If not for the cold I would have believed you
because in the summer everyone loves the gentle
breeze.
Close your eyes, they said,
And turn your face into the wind.
Nobody could have prepared me for the slap you
gave me across my cheek.
Your hypocrisy baffles me,
You blow in one direction only to blow in the
other moments later,
Always switching sides and going back on
yourself.
You say one thing and mean another,
You mean one thing and say the other,
I'm not sure which you I should believe.
You attention seeker.
Refusing to stop blowing until I pull my coat in
a little closer to my chest acknowledging your
existence.
You should win a BAFTA for the performances
you put on daily.
Sweeping the leaves from my path showing
yourself to be the perfect gentleman

Before blowing those same leaves in my face
when no one is looking.
Your inconsistency is tiring.
No one mentions your stutter to be polite,
But you are strong then weak,
Unpredictable and unreliable,
Subsiding for a moment before returning with
full force.
You blew me to the edge and blew out my flame.
Despite all this I'm grateful as you forced me to
build a house out of bricks so the wind couldn't
get in.

But it meant nothing else could either,
The price I pay in order to keep myself safe.

Between a Rock and a Hard Place

Geologists have a saying, rocks remember.
Daily I endure the weight of your body as you
walk all over me without a second thought as
though I was designed to bear the brunt.
You grow bored and kick me around, pick me up
and drop me,
And sometimes you skim me across the water
Seeing how many times I bounce back before
inevitably reaching rock bottom.
I told you I'd always be there for you and I
meant it,
But just because I rock does not mean I am
made of stone.
Sometimes I'm sedimentary and I break apart
and crumble just like you.
Just like you I'm not always rock solid.
I get tired of being told to stay firm.
I remember every time you sat on me during
every crisis as you reflect,
Never asking first if I can carry the weight of
your burdens before you cast them.
And where are you when I need you to hold me
down?
Who told you a rock feels no pain?

Instead I find you in a corner constantly
chipping me away,
You carve me into your ideal shape,
Forcing me to lose myself as I become what you
envisioned me to be.
If you insist on using me, then I ask that you rub
two of me together
Until you get a spark and a flame catches,
Give me a chance at love.
What do you think those before you did when
there were no matches?

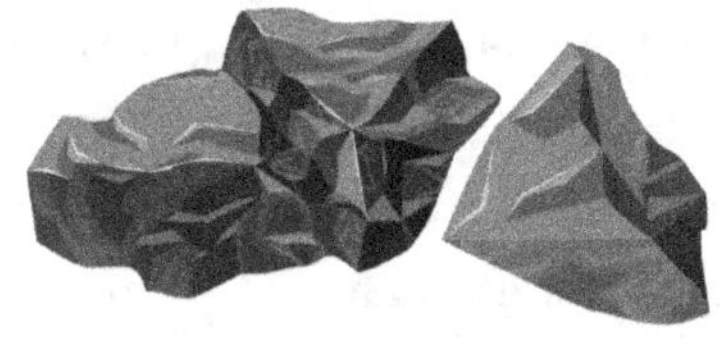

Another Rainy Day

If you were sky and I earth,
And everything in between were witness to our
love,
And God said you may now kiss the bride,
Would it rain?
If the rain were a demonstration of our love,
how heavy would it fall?
If at all.

But what if the rain were a demonstration of our
pain?
When would it stop?
Would the world grab tissues?
Why is it the sky can fall apart piercing its
shattered pieces
But the earth is expected to remain firm?
Bearing in mind when it rains it gets
everywhere.
A woman's love and a woman's patience was
always stronger than her counterpart
But God forbid she breaks.

Now imagine I were sky and you earth,
The moment it rained you would simply cease to
exist because you were never designed to handle
a woman's pain.

You coward!

Let There Be Light

To the sunshine I drew in the corner of every
white A4 page as a child,
I will wait for the moment you become whole
Because I can't love in quarters,
So come forth from your corner,
Let me love the whole of you,
I would set myself alight for you,

So come,
Let there be light.

The Sky Is Pink

Shafts of sunlight put the spotlight on me
So even in the middle of the day when I close
my eyes
There you were,
The sunset.
A vibrant blush of sky
Intensely coloured and tinted carnation pink.

Lost at Sea

I'm in Spain but the S is silent,
My screams are as loud as sirens,
But there is silence.

I'm so fucking tired of this life,
Last night I cried,
I cried into empty bottles to store my tears to use
for later because I know I will cry myself dry.
I know eventually those tears will form an ocean
so vast and so deep I will be lost forever.
My North is South and my East is West
And I am swimming in an ocean with no land in
sight
And all of a sudden I feel tired,
Like the world had left me no choice but to let
go.

That night I drowned myself in those very tears
that I shed,
That night the stars fell and I couldn't see,
That night I was lost at sea.

I got out of bed the next morning, mourning
All the thoughts I had the night before were still
swarming,

I look down and I see those tears on my pillow
case absorbing,
And in my dreams instead of soaring I saw
myself falling.
And even if my wings still work and I have just
enough strength to rise,
Underwater a bird cannot fly,
I'm trapped within the sea and beneath the sky.
And just when I think I can see the light,
I'm drowning again.

You have no idea how easy it is to fall back into
darkness.
Regardless of how hard I try, and how many
times you can count the sun rise
I never rise, and my world remains colourless,
And I often wonder how many suns I will have
to swallow to feel light.

I - Can't - Breathe
(underwater)

Loving you is like holding my breath
underwater.
I can't hold it forever but I can't let myself go.
Either way it's lose lose.
I - can't - breathe

you were snow.
f l a k y

dracarys

play stupid games. win
stupid prizes. play with fire
don't cry when you burn

Good Night

Light is easy to love,
Let me show you my darkness,
The innermost part of my soul,
My iris holds all my stories untold.
My eyes are mini night skies,
Each night both new and old cracks form and I
bleed light.
You call it scars, I call it stars,
Both alike, both formed from night.

Over the Moon -_-

You are the moon,
Unveiling the beauty of my darkness,
You love when my night comes out to play
For without me you have no depth,
Without me no one would look up at my night
sky and say look, the moon.
Without me there is no you.
I get it, if I were on earth I too would look at the
view.
But I hate it when you boast because at night
everyone looks up to you.
I always was your dark little secret,
So when you shun your light
You made it so bright that no one looks up at the
sky and sees the night.
Yet despite how many hearts you appease,
It's the night, then the moon.
Let me clarify.
It's me - before you.

Falling Star

If you could count the number of stars in the sky,
Would you count me, a falling one?
Would you make a wish?
Would you catch me as I collapse into myself
and burn to keep you warm,
And would you hold me still, as my flames burn
your skin, or would you drop me and watch me
fall to the point of no return.

If you could count the number of stars in the sky,
Would you play dot to dot as your fingers lead
you to mine
Creating a path that leads me to you.
Outline a map with coordinates and guide me to
the depths of your soul,
Don't you know light shines in dark places too,
So let me shine on you,
For the night is my home,
And this star isn't willing to give up the shadows
that created them.

If you could count the number of stars in the sky,
Would I be your constellation?
What would you name me?
And am I all that you see?

Or are there other constellations that catch your
gaze
Because when I look down on all that there is
You're the only thing that matters to me,
All other matter is simply debris.

The sky is never quite black enough so I can
show you my quintessential self in all my light
and beauty.
So when the sun goes down and all the stars
begin crystallising out of the dark blue ether of
dusk, you get lost looking for me.
But let me remind you, I am present without
presence.
And yet you cry so hard your horizon doubles,
over-running when it comes to the sky
And pain compels you to fall.
But deep calls out to deep.
The depth of your sorrow calls out to the depth
of my love
And out of your darkness I rise, and my light
runneth over falling out of the sky.

So I ask you once more,
If you could count the number of stars in the sky,
Would you count me, a falling one?

Leaf Me Alone

Have you ever thought about the journey of a
leaf?
I realised one morning that every single leaf has
its own story.
This particular leaf was green with jealousy,
Every time you walk past its bush and brush
your hand against its thighs you tease,
But you tease several leaves at the same time.
It doesn't mind but,
If only you knew how much it craves to be
touched; craves to be loved,
Prays that there's someone out there that gives a
fuck
It does not ask for much.
Only that you notice it.
One leaf amongst the many.
At first it may think its existence is collective
Then one faithful day out of the multitude, that
leaf was plucked,
It could not believe its luck,
The chosen one.
You can't tell because you hold it between your
finger and thumb
And by doing so it no longer has a will of its
own as it bends and folds at yours,

But it rejoices.
It rejoices because it was chosen.
It rejoices until you get bored of it and tear it
Not into two, no, but just enough that you've left
your mark,
A leaf never forgets its first tear.
You drop it on the ground where the rest of them
lie and go on with your life
After all, it is just a leaf,
There's plenty more on the tree.
But you should never pick up a leaf if you're just
going to play with it,
Instead you should let it keep growing.

Then comes along somebody else,
They see the leaf and pick it up,
Once again, it couldn't believe its luck.
On the battleground full of wounded soldiers it
was chosen.
This new person sees the tear and they promise
they could never do such a thing
As they proceed to patch it up and restore its
faith in humankind.
In its fragile state it opens itself up to be loved
again,
To trust again.
It knows what it felt like the first time and it
swore that would be its last,
As it did everything to make this last.

It even ignored the wind.
Imagine a leaf that does not dance to the tune of
the wind.
But like before, this person got bored, and tore.
It tore the leaf in the same place it swore it
would never tear,
Only this time, they tore a little more.
This cycle repeats itself until eventually the leaf
is torn into two.
Until the leaf has nothing left to lose.
Until you realise in the end, that leaf, is you.

Juniper Green

I have to live with the fact I said oui to the love
but you didn't mean we,
Our love it was never a tree it was more like a
leaf,
When all the stars fell, I couldn't see,
I feared for my life on a full moon when the
wolves came out to feast,
When it's dark at night I'm never at ease,
I burnt when I touched you and felt that you're
hot like 100°,
I froze like snow and was stiff in the knees,
I drowned when I swam for the key to your heart
that you threw in the sea,
Your sun rays stung like a venomous bee,
You always rain check when we're supposed to
meet,
If I tell you you rock would you stay grounded
for me?
But just like the wind, you've always got
somewhere to be.

Picture This

Everyday I stared at our photographs until the images blurred and my eyes were forced to blink because of the tears that filled them.
You wore a shade of my favourite colour and paired that with a subtle smile.
Unknown to me the cross I wore around my neck would later be used to comfort me from the red of my bandana that represented the blood that seeped through my broken heart.
I stared at them until my eyes began to burn and pain was the only thing that reminded me I was alive before I drew the first breath I'd taken in minutes because you literally took my breath away.
I had never liked anyone the way that I'd liked you.
I showed you my darkness and undressed my soul, laid naked before you I exposed all my vulnerabilities and destroyed the wall I built to let you in.
We were picture perfect but somehow I was replaced in our photographs with the image of another girl.
It made me question what was it about her that you didn't see in me, I hope she's someone who knows how rare it is to find someone like you,

And as my insecurities peaked, you removed the
colour that I had until I was a black and white
sketch that you rubbed out and painted over like
I was a blank canvas.
But my stars weren't willing to give up the
darkness that created them so now we're great
friends.
I printed out our photographs and drowned them
in water because that was the only way to make
you cry, so you would know what it felt like to
be drowned in tears.
The water was mixed with the tears that had
rolled across my cheeks, the same tears that
strangled my neck, suffocating making it hard
for me to breath.
Some of those tears made a pool in my dimples
because somehow I was happy that you found
someone you could love the same way they
loved you.
Some days I couldn't stop thinking about you,
and other days I wondered why I was wasting
my time.
And after a month of staring at our photographs,
I realised I found me the day that I lost you.
I set fire to our photographs and watched the
flame burn the corner of your stomach so you
could feel how the words "this won't go far" and
"I've got shit to do" made me sick.

I burnt the corner of your face because the only
face I had was the face of the reality that you
were never mine.
Even though I knew the circumstance we were
in meant we would never be, each day I spent
with you I hoped a little more that that would
change.
Even though you liked me it wasn't enough to
stop you from picking the other girl, and you
knew from that moment each day I spent with
you I was a naive little girl who spent her penny
on thoughts in movie screens that gave a false
sense of hope.
I burnt those corners so I could live outside the
box of our photographs,
Live outside the poem I wrote you titled "Until
Next Time" because I realised there wouldn't be
a next time.
But all we ever see of stars are their old
photographs.
And at the end I understood,
We got close when it was your time to leave, so
now I've got to let you go.

The Long Way Home

The train journey back was quiet. Nothing could be heard except the chugging sound and the occasional whistle that sounded like a forlorn call in the night. I had finally accepted that I had overstayed my welcome and it was time for me to go back home. Home - after all is where the heart is and my heart was missing its familiar belonging. But there is always an air of sadness when you have to leave a place you love so much. Love - is like a two-edged sword, it cuts you when it comes and it cuts you when it leaves. Either way you bleed. One teardrop followed after another, each of them hitting the same distressed note as they hit the interior flooring of the train. They formed a small puddle at my feet. I pressed my face against the window and closed my eyes. I remembered something that I'd read the other day, "Darkness doesn't last forever. Even when you close your eyes, the light can still get in". I opened them again and watched the leaves fall to the tune of the wind. I ought to take a leaf out of nature's book and learn the art of letting go. If the trees can laugh, why can't I? After all, this process is all a part of life. The Greek philosopher Heraclitus once said, "The only thing that is constant is change" and I guess he was right. So much change has occurred in my life. I adapted to change and adopted it. Constantly changing my rhythm as each new person walked in and out of my life. So, if I can fall in love, I should have no problem falling out of it too. Right? There is an impermanency to life where nothing lasts forever and I know that now. I continued to look out the window. The sky was a special shade of blue. The summer petals have browned, soon to join a garland of scarlets and golds. The youth of nature has taken a seat to allow a renewal. I would like to think of my heart in the same light. To remold something, you must first break it, and my heart has already been broken too many times. Laughter soft as tears fills my mouth in the hope of a brighter tomorrow, and that after darkness does come light.

have a nice life

a hole where you used
to be. they told me you moved
on. that's news to me